T0413558

SEA LAMPREYS

BY TRUDY BECKER

Apex is distributed by North Star Editions:
sales@northstareditions.com | 888-417-0195

Produced for Apex by Red Line Editorial.

Photographs ©: Jelger Herder/Buiten-Beeld/Alamy, cover, 22–23, 24; Shutterstock Images, 1, 19, 21, 26–27; Jill DeVito/iNaturalist, 4–5; A. Miehls/Great Lakes Fishery Commission, 6–7, 8–9; T. Lawrence/Great Lakes Fishery Commission, 10–11; iStockphoto, 12–13; Kasia Mullett/USFWS, 14; Stephen Domeracki/Great Lakes Science Center/USGS, 15, 29; Great Lakes Fishery Commission, 16–17; Nature and Science/Alamy, 18; US Fish and Wildlife Service, 20; Blickwinkel/A. Hartl/Alamy, 25

Library of Congress Control Number: 2024944597

ISBN
979-8-89250-321-1 (hardcover)
979-8-89250-359-4 (paperback)
979-8-89250-433-1 (ebook pdf)
979-8-89250-397-6 (hosted ebook)

Printed in the United States of America
Mankato, MN
012025

NOTE TO PARENTS AND EDUCATORS

Apex books are designed to build literacy skills in striving readers. Exciting, high-interest content attracts and holds readers' attention. The text is carefully leveled to allow students to achieve success quickly. Additional features, such as bolded glossary words for difficult terms, help build comprehension.

TABLE OF CONTENTS

CHAPTER 1

TiME TO EAT

A sea lamprey floats in Lake Huron. The lamprey is looking for food. Soon, a trout moves past. The sea lamprey swims toward the larger fish.

A sea lamprey must wriggle and bend its whole body to move through water.

The lamprey sinks its teeth into the trout. The trout tries to shake it off. But the lamprey holds tight.

FAST FACT

Sea lampreys have tongue-like body parts. These parts can scrape through fish scales.

A sea lamprey's mouth has several rings of sharp teeth.

The lamprey begins to suck up the trout's blood. It drinks for days. The trout gets weaker and weaker. Finally, the lamprey lets go. It swims away to find its next **host**.

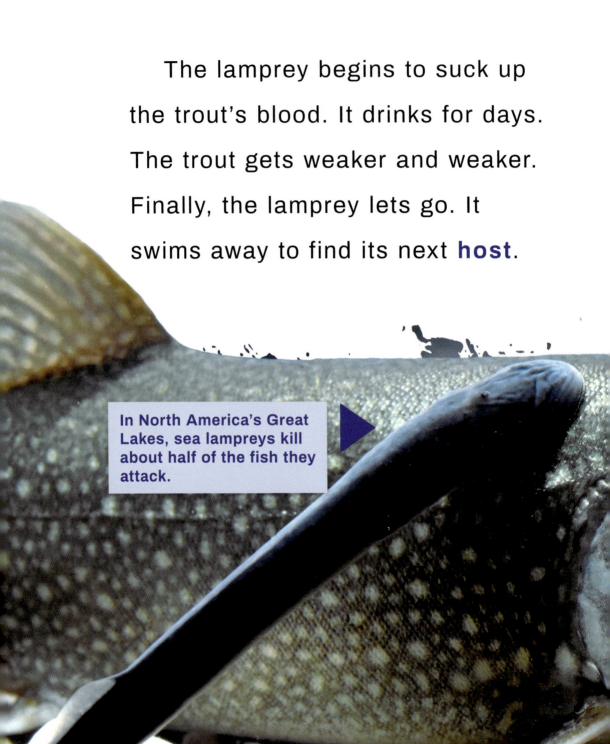

In North America's Great Lakes, sea lampreys kill about half of the fish they attack.

DRINK UP

After attaching to a host, a sea lamprey lets out a chemical from its mouth. The chemical stops the host's blood from **clotting**. That way, the lamprey can keep drinking.

CHAPTER 2

LARGE LAMPREYS

Lampreys are fish with long bodies. These fish have **cartilage** instead of bones. Some sea lampreys grow nearly 4 feet (1.2 m) long.

Lampreys have no scales. Instead, they have smooth skin.

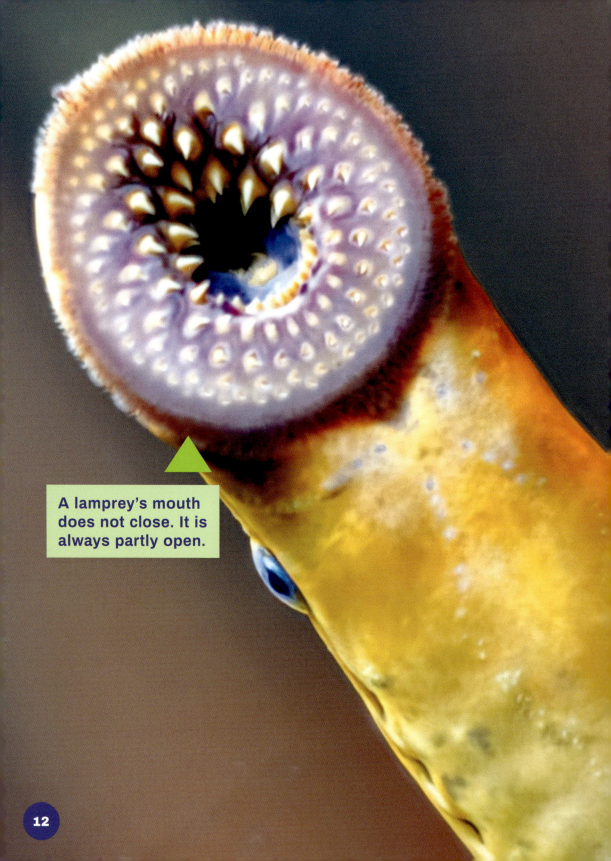

A lamprey's mouth does not close. It is always partly open.

A sea lamprey has a large, round mouth. The mouth works like a **suction cup**. It lets the lamprey hold tightly to a host.

FAST FACT

A sea lamprey has more than 100 teeth.

Sea lampreys do best in cool water. They are **native** to the Atlantic Ocean. But they have spread to several large lakes.

Scientist sometimes use chemicals to kill lampreys and keep them from spreading.

In the early 2020s, hundreds of thousands of sea lampreys lived in the Great Lakes.

NEW WATERS

In the 1800s, people built large canals in the United States. The waterways connected the Atlantic Ocean to the Great Lakes. Sea lampreys swam through the canals. They found new places to live.

CHAPTER 3

BLOOD SUCKERS

Sea lampreys are **parasites**. They suck blood from living hosts. Sometimes, the hosts survive. But they often die.

Several sea lampreys may feed on the same fish.

Sea lampreys leave marks after they let go of fish.

Even when host fish don't die right away, sea lamprey attacks cause several problems. Hosts often get sick. They may become too weak to have babies or escape from **predators**.

One sea lamprey can kill 40 pounds (18 kg) of fish in its lifetime.

The problems are often worse when lampreys spread to new areas. For example, lampreys have few predators in the Great Lakes. They have killed many native fish there.

Each year, sea lampreys kill nearly 10 million pounds (4.5 million kg) of fish in the Great Lakes.

In Europe, native catfish eat sea lampreys.

IN DANGER

Sea lampreys in Europe don't kill as many fish. In fact, those lampreys are in danger of dying out. More predators eat them. Humans catch and eat them. People have also polluted the water. That makes it harder for lampreys to live.

CHAPTER 4

LAMPREY LIFE

Sea lampreys start their lives in rivers or streams. **Larvae** float downstream. Then, they dig into the sand. They eat tiny pieces of plants and animals that sink to the bottom.

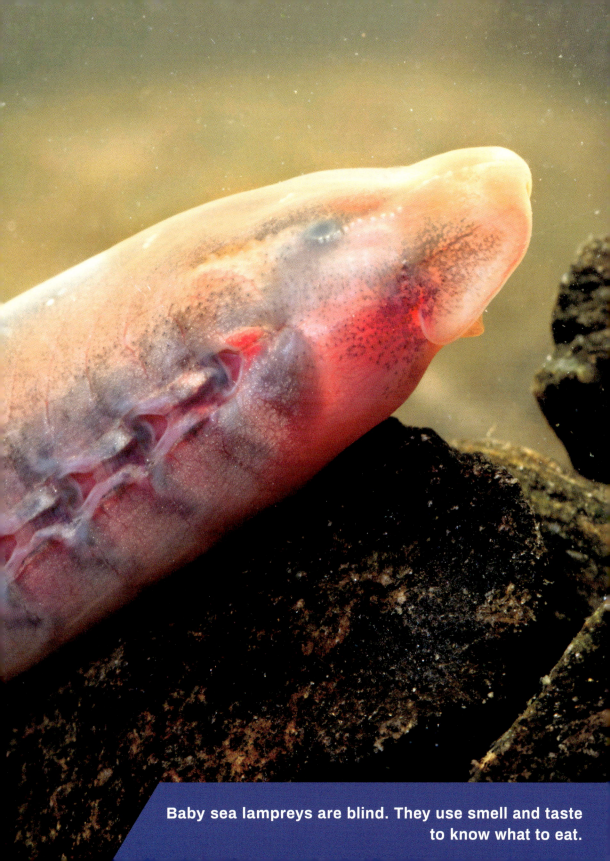

Baby sea lampreys are blind. They use smell and taste to know what to eat.

Next, larvae grow eyes and larger, rounder mouths. They swim into the sea or deeper into freshwater lakes. The **juvenile** lampreys begin to find hosts.

When they are larvae, lampreys can only live in freshwater rivers and streams.

Sea lampreys live for about six years in the wild.

GROWING UP

Sea lampreys grow slowly. Some spend more than five years as larvae. Then, their juvenile phase usually lasts one or two years.

Finally, sea lampreys become adults. They return to streams and rivers. Females lay eggs. Both parents die soon after.

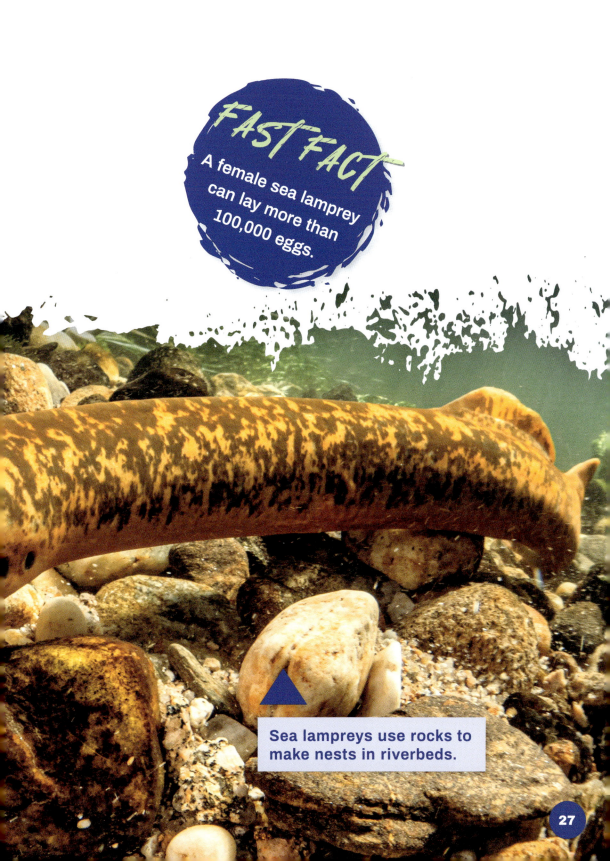

FAST FACT

A female sea lamprey can lay more than 100,000 eggs.

Sea lampreys use rocks to make nests in riverbeds.

COMPREHENSION *QUESTIONS*

Write your answers on a separate piece of paper.

1. Write a few sentences explaining the main points of Chapter 3.

2. What do you think is the scariest part of a sea lamprey? Why?

3. What part of fish do sea lampreys feed on?

   A. blood

   B. cartilage

   C. bones

4. Why would lampreys kill more fish in places with fewer predators?

   A. More of the lampreys would die young.

   B. The lampreys would hunt less.

   C. The lampreys would live longer and find more hosts.

5. What does **survive** mean in this book?

*They suck blood from living hosts. Sometimes, the hosts **survive**. But they often die.*

   A. pass away
   B. move quickly
   C. continue to live

6. What does **phase** mean in this book?

*Sea lampreys grow slowly. Some spend more than five years as larvae. Then, their juvenile **phase** usually lasts one or two years.*

   A. a part of an ocean
   B. a step in a life cycle
   C. a time of day

Answer key on page 32.

GLOSSARY

cartilage

Tissue that is softer and more bendable than bone.

clotting

Sticking together to form a thick clump.

host

An animal that another animal attaches to and feeds on.

juvenile

A young animal that is not a baby but is not fully grown.

larvae

Animals that have hatched from eggs but have not yet changed to juveniles or adults.

native

Originally living in an area.

parasites

Animals or plants that live on or in other living things.

predators

Animals that hunt and eat other animals.

suction cup

An object that can stick to surfaces.

TO LEARN MORE

BOOKS

Downs, Kieran. *Barracuda vs. Moray Eel*. Minneapolis: Bellwether Media, 2022.

Huddleston, Emma. *Food Chains*. Minneapolis: Abdo Publishing, 2022.

Walker, Tracy Sue. *Saving Endangered Species*. Minneapolis: Lerner Publications, 2024.

ONLINE RESOURCES

Visit **www.apexeditions.com** to find links and resources related to this title.

ABOUT THE AUTHOR

Trudy Becker lives in Minneapolis, Minnesota. She likes exploring new places and loves anything involving books.

INDEX

ANSWER KEY:
1. Answers will vary; 2. Answers will vary; 3. A; 4. C; 5. C; 6. B